I0623308

Anything You Want

Christopher Sawyer-Lauçanno

Wet Cement Press

Asheville, Berkeley, Reno

Anything Your Want ©2024
by Christopher Sawyer-Lauçanno
ISBN 979-8-9918692-1-8

Library of Congress Control Number:
2025931566

All rights reserved. No portion of this work
may be reproduced or transmitted in any form,
or by any means, electronic or mechanical,
without prior permission in writing from Wet
Cement Press.

The gate is open

Cover artwork by Anthony Schlagel.
Back cover watercolor by Christopher
Sawyer-Lauçanno, from *Learning to Use Black*.

Wet Cement Press
1908 Yolo Ave
Berkeley, CA 94707

www.wetcementpress.com

Anything You Want

> The quiet advances
> as best it can, until my voice
> is able to reach me....

Christopher Sawyer-Lauçanno was a person of many lives, not only in his prolific and fecund outpouring of imagination, nor in all the countries he traveled and lived, studied and wrote—nor the innumerable people he counseled and taught, but also in the many moments when he walked up to the edge of death—only to surprise us all and come back to write another brilliant book, as he has in gifting us yet one more to cherish in *Anything You Want*. In the realm of his poetic manifestations over five decades, *Anything You Want* stands as his magnum opus, a final salutation of gratitude to all he experienced and loved, and to all of us who love him. In pulling forth his immense chi and vitality of mind and heart, he managed—under often quite dire physical conditions—to reveal the mystery and secret of his bountiful creativity by fully exploring spheres beyond life and death, or coming and going, in a verse that simultaneously invents and forges koans for us who lament his passing, and in the end for us to discover, the ole maestro hasn't gone anywhere after all:

> East, west, north, south
> everything is all right,
> everything is all right or not all right,
> only for me, everything is all right.

Those lines from the Zen master, Quingliang (Fayan Wenyi) were among Christopher's favorites, and he often quoted them to me in our daily letters and koan exchanges that began after he was first diagnosed with cancer over a decade ago. A quiet Zen master of his own making, Christopher embodied the meaning of this koan with an indefatigable gusto and cheer, frequently reminding me of what one of his teachers had once said to him when he and his family were living in Japan:

Teacher, I am discouraged, what should I do? Encourage others, his teacher responded.

And that's what Christopher did: encouraged, coached, or consoled the countless writers and friends who came to him for council with their own books, creative projects, or illnesses, or despair with the world's plight, or those of their own personal lives. In some ways, Quingliang's "only for me, everything is all right" echoes Chris' fierce passion for life with his cherished family—and in his own poems, translations, and stories, as well as in his social and political convictions over a lifetime of caring for the world, its environment, social justice and equity, and everyone he met, taught and from whom he continuously learned:

> Moments rearrange themselves
> as they will:
> upside down, slantwise, trapezoidal
> Each has its own beauty
> its own perfect symmetry

How he found that beauty and symmetry is, in large part, what *Anything You Want* invites us to find out for ourselves. It's also, in part, revealed in what he learned from another of his friends and teachers, Peter Matthiessen, who once said to him: "Our purpose in life is to help others through it." With his beloved wife and partner in all things, the extraordinary poet, Patricia Pruitt, together they supported and nurtured a network of writers and artists around the globe—from Paris & Tangier to Tokyo & Istanbul—and often hosted readings and salons in their welcoming home (or "grass hut" as Chris liked to refer to it) once they settled in Turners Falls. Theirs is a great love story. Christopher and Patricia were renowned in the town and active in every aspect of the town and county's life. They participated in as well as created communities.

And as Lawrence Ferlinghetti once remarked while introducing Chris at City Lights in San Francisco: "Christopher is famous among the famous." So many of us were continuously amazed by his stories about the influential thinkers and writers he'd spent time with on his continuous pilgrimages around the globe. He was a poet, translator, biographer, librettist, memoirist, painter, architect, scholar, professor, and pianist as well as a fabulous cook.

> The eye and ear
> and occasionally the nose
> or tongue or skin
> creates the ligatures
> that bind phenomena to us...

This book, and indeed, his whole life, is a testament to the power of poetry, of all forms of creative imaginings, and he lived it with humility, kindness, simplicity, a deep joie de vivre and with profound wisdom and a lively and generous sense of humor.

In *Anything You Want* you will find these characteristics chiseled through time and timelessness with a precision rarely sustained in language's infinite potential for revealing both the reality of everyday life and what the poet Osip Mandelstam once called: "the what should be." The poems wander through the realms of birth and death, loss and abundance, radical acceptance and on further through the smallest miraculous details of tenderness for how we live with and help one another. He wrote them for us with verve, compassion, meditation, and in continuous practice, in spite of his increasing weakness this past year while approaching his final departure from the body. In this way, the poems, too, become koans for discovering and welcoming the questions of our own life, and the miracles waiting to be found. Chris would encourage that, as he encouraged countless others, to dive more fully into the beauty and poetry of their own lives.

This verse is a complete emergence into an imagination beyond imagination.

As in a poem by Thich Nhat Hanh, who Chris also frequently quoted, Thay writes:

This body cannot contain me,
I am in the flow of this calm mind,
I am life without boundaries.
I have never been born,
And I will never die.
Over there, the wide sea,
And sky with countless galaxies,
All manifestations on the basis of awareness.

From beginningless time, we have always been free.
Birth and death is just a door
Through which we come and go.
Birth and death is just a game
Of hide and seek.
So smile, wave hello, goodbye, hello again.
We are always meeting again
In our true nature.
We are always meeting again,
In the myriad flow of life.

Thank you, Christopher.
We're always meeting.

John Ninso High
Lisbon
November 1, 2024

For Imogene Pruitt-Spence
and
In Memoriam Patricia Pruitt

"Anything you want."

—Octavio Paz responding to a question about what his poems mean. Harvard, 1974

"Writers don't own their words. Since when do words belong to anybody? 'Your very own words,' indeed! And who are you?"

—Brion Gysin, *Let the Mice In*

"Words are how we understand the koans. But who knows whether the words actually convey what some old master said? And who really knows what the words really are trying to say? A paradox as great as any koan. So what do we do? Point our fingers at the moon."

—Monk Goan to Patricia Pruitt, Daihonzan Kofuskusan Kenchouji, Kamakura, Japan, 1981

Anything You Want

In a different manner
veering toward the light,
away from shadows halting
then going on without us.
A shadow world without disruption.

There seems to be little difference
between drowsiness and wakefulness.
just the striking coincidence
of a no or two piled on top of a yes.

Mind does not provide a solution.
Not sure the body does either.
A weak, old voice somewhere
seemingly in the distance
but also inside.
All but inaudible except
for a phrase here and there.

And what does one hear?
Single syllables. Traces of words.
A sound before sound?
All pointing backward,
or inward, or outward.

Whatever it is that
fabulates multiple mysteries
out of what should be ordinariness,
engenders a mental landscape
of a jumbly packed
within another jumbly.

Etymology fails.
All we can do is cut
through concordant sound,
make tonality sing for us
without a need to understand.

The quiet advances
as best it can, until my voice
is able to reach me.

Now it's just a matter
of extracting the verbs
from nouns
and excessive adverbial gestures.

Disinterring static
un-remembrance
from a forgotten burial
of old awareness,
upends the ash bin
of not-knowing.

Now in the emergence
we can see and feel
and even perhaps hear
in our mouth's ear
what we long ago
decided to forget.

In moving among
the afterglow of shapes,
those artifacts of the imagined,
or perhaps actual
world, that once
presented itself
to the senses,
a rather curious
confrérie emerges
between one object
and then another,
one memory and then another,
the way an adjective
helps determine
what it is we once felt
what we once believed
to be absolutely true.

Names interlope,
gain a certain potency
even if we fail to recognize
their frail substance.

Counting syllables is futile,
searching for stresses
is only a game played
for our own amusement.

Best to take the signs
as they come,
realize they are not
calling out to us.

They just are.

Moments rearrange themselves
as they will:
upside down, slantwise, trapezoidal.

Each has its own beauty,
its own perfect symmetry.

Jolts of recognition
prevail despite
our surprise at how
the minuscule universe
has suddenly rearranged itself.

In the *Upanishads* we find this:
"By the word alone
is the non-word revealed."

Language is the way in
to non-language,
even though occasionally
we would jettison
words to arrive directly
in a place beyond linguistic
cacophonous confusion.

Such vainglory:
Writing words in an
attempt to reveal
the non-word.

To transpose actualities,
to discover that a ghost lives,
or that bee pollen collects on trees.

Bend back the artifice,
rearrange the demonstrable
denotations until they
become connotations.

Metaphor triumphs over metonymy
even if the original question gets blurred,
and the answer, even if one exists,
becomes lost in a whirl of possibilities.

Outside the dahlias bloom,
admire themselves,
offer up their splendor
to the newborn sun.
Leaves leaf on the trees
signaling that all is well,
at least for the moment.

Inside are dark, unvisited places
where cats enjoy roaming,
where beetles burrow,
where mice rear their heads,
cock their ears for danger
and sniff the air
looking for a tasty bite
unattended.

New words dragged
up from old lexicons,
hang on a flimsy filament,
that stretches back in time,
their once homes
in distant places buried
beneath layers of additions
piled on editions.

Our tongues still twist
around those ancient songs.

As in:

Old Frisian *word*
Old Dutch *wort*
Old Saxon *word*
Middle Low German *wort*

As in the definition of Word:
"a speech sound
or series of speech sounds
that symbolizes and communicates
a meaning usually without
being divisible into smaller
units capable of independent use."

And:
"a single distinct meaningful element of
speech or writing."

As in: Chaucer's *Pardoner's Tale:*
"Now wol I speke of oothes false and grete
A word or two, as olde bokes trete.

The recognizing eye
is also recognized
as perspective snaps in and out.
In the early morning light,
generating nodes produce
a solar geometry,
a hypotenuse triangle
in which reciprocation
between the seen
and self emerges.

The line of maples is not
an accessory nor a prop
for gaze to sight
but fundamental
to each glance
outward and inward:
A kind of curious satisfaction
satisfying itself
at our expense.

Air quite still, shut in, shut out
dust gathers,
as does the cloud moving
somewhere in the dark,
searching for a smidge of light.

Moving deliberately this morning
amid myriad artifacts
gathered over time
and then even more time,

enclosed in one's own making,
collecting, acquiring,
a way of remembering a past
but also forgetting a present.

Not stopped but not advancing either,
just resting in place, waiting.
But for what? Some reason
to go forward or to retreat?
A prod more compelling than
our old friend, stasis?

Here, fixed, anticipating
a sign of some sort
that tells us how to do
what we are already doing?

Or are we expecting
something even larger
that forces us to move
in whatever direction
the wind is blowing?

Is it simply about fitting
form to purpose
or purpose finding
the form it needs
to express itself?

Either way words get
tangled up in the process,
convey or obscure
density and depth.

A way of putting it.
A way of recovering it.

Even when iterating syllables
rushing toward enunciation
are not necessarily the ascension
we had anticipated.

Unwelcome distortions
can result in happy mistakes
that send the syntax reeling
into a host of new metaphors,
contextual possibilities
indicating that something impossible,
encased only in language may exist.

We would like to have something
meaningful to say,
a pronouncement worthy
of the long horizon that beckons
us to move forward.

But we are tongue-tied
at exactly the moment
when we should be speaking
to the sunlight that is creating
pools of light between
the river and the tree-lined
shore beyond.

Perhaps, that is the
only articulation we need.
It has already embodied itself
in our phrasing
that refuses to arrive
as words derived
from our ears and eyes.

Conspicuous similarities linger
between latent and patent:
a vindication, we might say,
of flagrant anachronisms.

At that crossroads when and where
nothing prompts us to understand
despite countless glossaries
and all-night guesswork.

Systematized codification
once our bolt-hole,
somehow, somewhere
got tossed out the window.

Anecdotal detail is
left for the recognizing eye,
but incredulity continues to abound.

Equilibrium is elusive,
odd vectors pull against each other,
create both attraction and repulsion.

Colliding forces bounce
from corner to corner,
impeding an easy walk along the path.

Yet nothing is visible in the chill,
just a few clouds we hope will part,
allow us to go for a stroll,

take in the early morning air,
smile at the scattering squirrels,
pay homage to a less complicated

arrangement of force against force,
allow for movement forward of any sort.
Instead, we are left squirming in our armchairs.

Return
turns
inward
as a breach in the wall
comforts
a passageway.

ebb
flow
flux

and fixity
purloined by any stream
placate the nomadic impulse

A rooster crows before dawn.
A dog barks.
The gate is open.

Echoes vanish
before they are born.
Wordlessness clings to old lichens.

Another kind of quiet
is born from the intersection
of day and night.

The fading sun hovers
over the distant ridge
and a cold moon
decorates the sky.

We cannot rise above the ashes
of our own cinders.

The left behind dogs us
even as the arms and legs grow weak.

Leave something for tomorrow
to recall some yesterday or some today.
The iron gets hammered on the anvil

becomes form for our longings.

The days grow dimmer:
darkness visible means
no light at all

Today is only a specific point
in our own time out of time
a midway place
in the midst of a miasma.

Perhaps Hippocrates was right.
It is just the air breezing
from some locale
to which we should not venture
that makes us weak, then weaker.

A moment in time only.
The wrong moment in place.

Denotation flows into connotation,
then back again,
so that the arrangement
of pointing passes
outward and inward,
not so unlike
our own crooked finger
pointing to a distant constellation.

Hints of remembrance
cluster at the tail ends of imagination
shift shapes, bend into vagueness,
teeter on obscurity's brink.

Decipherment is difficult
but descriptors still emerge
as connected or
ajar as pigeons in a square.

We once saw
this or that, knelt here,
stumbled there,
gripped the ladder rungs,
stood still in the snow.

Vital questions
never enunciated to the air
reappear again and again.

Answers are not returned.

The failure of inconsistency
to be consistent
often results in insightful
or wrong-headed misunderstandings.

As when possibilities trip
over one another
because the parchment
has been pieced together.

Tatters and gaping holes emerge
from what was once a pristine whole.
Words, some intact, some missing,
entire sentences erased by
neglect or maybe just hungry mice
force our minds to make new,
though the preferred term is "re-creation."

No longer scribes but compositors,
we freely invent missing phrases
to provide a way for
some sort of sense to emerge.

And then the new
rubs off on us
the way ink stains fingers.
Fragments get turned

into wholeness because
we can't abide not knowing.

Parsing particulars is as useless
as asking a cow to moo on cue.
Both convergent and divergent traits
are apparent within an otherwise
indissoluble combination.

Each disjuncture is enshrouded
Within brevity and accuracy
well beyond the realm
of any imaginative
mathematical formula.

What do we do then
with avid circularity,
where elliptic implications abound?

As in: the snake swallowing its tail.

There is a certain vitality
present in the abrupt change
from day into night,
just as the difference is acute
between disproportion distracting
you from the gradual growing belief
that you and this very moment are one.

Interloping instances abound,
steer us away from what
we used to think was resolve
to harness our desire
for understanding.

Our intent now is as allusive
as those cluttered jottings
that have become
indecipherable.
What we originally intended
as reminders
of something we might
otherwise forget are as useless
as a scribbled grocery list.

Deterred from whatever
it was we were trying to do,
our mission not any longer
of much use,
just a heap of accretions,
unimportant deflections,
hardly a deciphering metaphysics
for exploring the unknowable.

Clear sight traces the formation
of what once were silhouettes
precariously perched on the edge
of the yawning void.

You struggle to explain
the what and why to yourself,
conjure up a flimsy reason
for what is now long gone.

Perhaps you were simply
groping within the dark,
seeking some affirmation
that absence still
has a vital existence.

Preferring regretting,
preferring loss
to knowing that nothing
actually ever went quietly
slinking away into the air.

Profundity never laid in ambush
waiting for me to arrive
at a desolate crossroad.

But a rooster, that I mentally
converted into a fighting cock,
once chased me into a ditch.

Later I thought I could have won big
if I'd fixed spurs to that bantam
and hauled it behind the bullring.

Now I've only got
a little dog barking
to go for a walk.

It's somewhere like there
we're trying to get to
but with lame walking,
blind stepping, bird hopping...

You see how it is.

This is what I was
trying to understand.
This is what I thought
I could understand.

But then
the sun went down
and the bushes got creepy
and the branches got wild
and the idea of path
got as tangled
as memory.

The completing words do not appear,
Because you still believe in barriers
believe that time arcs in the moonlight.

You haven't yet grasped
that time is not separate from you,
not marked by coming and going.
the moment you went out of the gate
you swallowed up time
and time swallowed you.

Unforeseen events countered
all of our predictions,
made a mockery of our staunch belief
that all would keep going on as it had,
albeit with a wrinkle or two.
Self-assurances were only wishes
founded on just because.

We are becoming accustomed
to sequences of hospitable intervals
in which lists of necessities
prevail over wants.

There is no way around
acceptance, no way out
from an undercover haven.
Instability is not a mutation
of what used to pass for orderliness.

It is its own order, rising up
to embrace us, day in and day out.

"Observes and then continues to observe,"
said Stevens.

Which is a way of saying
what a poem does
(or a poet does either awake or sleeping).

Exemplars depleted of dexterity
still shine when the light hits them
at the right moment,
makes them seem almost exotic,
as when walking through the woods
on a cold morning and suddenly
the sun sends its rays
bouncing through the branches.

Just moments to remember,
to take in as we can or will,
to puzzle before we move on.

Small full words
within the fabric
of big confusing words,
both capable of assigning
meaning to gesture
gesture to meaning
but in ways that differ,
or at times converge
when we least expect them too.

A way of saying
Anglo-Saxon never totally
bowed down to French.

Another way of saying it
is that language is not a vocabulary
that sits beautifully boxed on a shelf
but the ongoing shaping and reshaping,
the making and remaking,
the evoking and revoking
of what we previously said with it.

Listening to the birds
talk to each other this morning
I seem to hear bursts of emotion
rising between them, within me,
perhaps true, perhaps just feigned.

Emphatically phatic,
caws become shrieks,
trills give way to warbles,
cheeps are answered with peeps.

Terminological confusion
or discontinuous expansion
fills the air, and yet
the conversation is
as apparent as the dead leaves
falling in their free variations.

Coincidences of the visible universe:
A robin in the snow
on a dark afternoon,
come north too soon;
blue skies and rain;
my left foot moving along
behind the right.

The wordless world is framed
by language, in language.
Arbitrariness becomes a pattern,
makes us believe that discourse
is not dissonant nor false
even if it hasn't yet arrived
in our perplexed vocabularies.

And then there is
the immediate intimacy
of waking in a strange bed
in a strange town
and hearing the same birds
singing in the same trees,
or hearing the rain
come down
in the same manner
as it did elsewhere.

Perhaps we place far
too much importance
on decipherment, on somehow
being able to understand
the world behind the world,
or the word behind the word.

What does it really get us
but a devious or deviant
chain of transmission?

It's just another method
of flawed pattern making.
Some consolation,
I suppose, even in that.

How now to proceed
against the roaring tide
sweeping in upon the shore
threatening to pull us under?

Against the roaring tide
we flounder in the waves
threatening to pull us under
struggling to maintain ourselves.

We flounder in the waves
struggling to maintain ourselves.
Night begins to fall
and we cease to worry.

Struggling to maintain ourselves
we cease to worry
let go of our presumptions
wrap caution in a kiss.

We cease to worry
wrap caution in a kiss,
wade in to the words
welcome each caress.

Wrap caution in a kiss,
Welcome each caress
Of waves of words
threatening to pull us under.

An austere codifier,
just the elaboration
of a dismissed echo,
lurks out of sight,
ready to declaim words
with their meanings jumbled.

A direct statement waits
somewhere off stage, ready
to make its entrance,
unceremoniously.
but with diction
fused to perception.

Random scribal marks,
even those not yet revealed
to carry associations,
still cause the tongue
to place itself
in a variety of positions
within the mouth
so that distinct sounds
may emerge.

Basic oppositions determine
the determiner,
unless, of course,
there is nothing to determine.

We can't determine
whether it will rain or snow,
only whether we
should venture forth.

I'm determined to stay put,
save myself from determination
of which path to follow.

The armchair beckons
with greater resolve
than the world outside.
Inside is also a kind of outside.

Perhaps tomorrow
when the sun
is supposed to shine
my dog and I

will get up the gumption
to follow our feet
or our paws into
the known unknown.

The river below is cast in shadow,
though sun illuminates the hills.
My little dog cavorts upon the grass,
rolling now and then within the green,
taking care to avoid even the slightest stone,
not caring too much to roam.

I have more than a little desire to roam,
move well beyond my looming shadow,
not remain as fixed as a tree or stone,
wander up and beyond the hills,
seek out new varieties of green,
discover new flowers and fresh grass.

I long, like Rimbaud, to walk barefoot on the
    grass
follow my feet wherever they care to roam,
knowing that I will not stay within the green
but find light and dark and lengthening
    shadow,
as I stride and strut up and down the hills,
not fastened to earth as is a stone.

Maybe I'll rest for a while perched on a stone,
then refreshed, traipse through the bending
    grass,
following the birds that call from distant hills,
happy to wander, to be, to roam
without fear of the dark or of any shadow
even when I can no longer see the green.

Green, oh how I love you, green,
even the moss that gathers on a stone,
that changes its color in light and shadow,
as does each waving blade of grass,
I encounter each moment as I roam,
within the valley between the hills.

The stream flows downward from the hills
its water changing from blue to green.
Along its gently winding banks I roam
hoping to cross by hopping from stone to
    stone,
to alight on the other side amidst new grass,
feel the new light before the descending
    shadow.

In the glade the peaks cast their shadow,
causing me to pause, content now not to
    roam
just gaze in wonder at trees and shrubs and
    grass.

Long ago we recognized
that sameness was not possible
but we didn't plan for catastrophe,
didn't ready the lifeboats
or scrawl the number
of the fire department
on the back of our hands.

Phantasms arise from the deep,
confounding the very nature
of what we once thought true.
Only fragments remain
of what we used to believe
to be a whole.

And then the great paradox enters
as forthright as Fortinbras
cleaning up Hamlet's mess.

A strange illusion—the once world
of our imagination—
made even stranger by our inability
to colonize it as it actually was,
yielding a present freedom to recreate
as we will, how we will, when we will.

Everything becomes possible again,
facts can skew to our liking,
and now in the remembering is a definite
   absence
of grim upheavals or outlandish detours.

Still, of course, a tidy illusion
a non-existent figment.

The given world
is here
not over there,
an amorphism
not bound
by our best intentioned
expressive efforts
of how we see it
or how we say it.

It just is and could care
less than two hoots
about how we perceive
or characterize it.

All of that
is simply for us
to feel some definition
of ourselves, of others,
to ignore, if we choose,
the exquisite power
of the leafing oak tree
towering just to tower.

In the ongoing
quest for our
very own ὀμφαλός,
we only find pebbles,
of various sizes,
rounded by the water
lapping over them
through time.

I suppose these
smooth rocks
could be construed
as our own navels
of the found world.
Which is a way of saying
our Delphi is right here,
right now.

With the force of axioms,
lavish gestures, scarcely
waiting to succumb,
become genuine preoccupations.

Burdens do not want to dwindle
just for the sake of dwindling.
Will the present formulation overcome
my hesitancy at decisiveness?

I have been trading in moribund calculations
for a long time now.

Words blown away in someone's desert.

Anything you want
you may have
but you don't want anything
you can put your finger on,
or even enumerate aloud.

Small triumphs make you feel cozy,
allow you to remove the lap blanket
for a minute or two.

So the days go, and the nights, too,
even though you can't fall asleep with ease.

So many words rush in, thoughts multiply
resulting in useless verbal investigations
of antiquated meanings:

Is a "mot" the sound a forloyn makes?
Or do the two words both indicate
the shrill note produced by a bugle?

And how did we choose
at some point after 1066
to retain "word" over "mot?"

All these musings for nothing
mostly forgotten in the first light.

The ordinary given is emptied,
has made way for thingness,
becomes exalted,
as if it were a thing.

A quiet universe of appearances
stands in for solidity,
only to be suffused
into the abstractions of the abstract.

It goes something like this:
elemental paradigms
wandering at will
within the sententious
accumulation of still
phrases move
space into time,
time into space.

Though we may not realize it,
we are free to grasp
or not grasp
the array of possibilities
scattered before us.

As if held up,
fixed within habitual
placements and place,
simply another element
in some chemical reaction,
not a catalyst.

We make lists
so we can remember
to remember,
scratch items off
whether completed
or just because they
don't matter any longer,
add others that we feel
are required by some
heretofore and so important
overlooked necessity,
then realize that maybe
none of this matters much at all.

Begin again.

It's tempting to equate
reason and order
with the way we arrange
one word after another,
and yet we are not under
any obligation
to affix non-sense
to sense
or sense to non-sense.

But because they are words,
and we are accustomed
to believe that words
carry meaning,
we want to recognize
each syllabic alignment
as forming understanding.

How to make an anything
out of a something
or a nothing?

A quandary worthy of Parmenides.

In the spring air a welter of sounds
of monotonous commonness,
but all seems exactly as it should.
There is hardly a need for fixation
on unrealizable aspirations.

Naiveté is a plausible excuse
to extend this lack of foresight.

Downhill or uphill mean
only the direction
in which we're going.

The eye and ear
and occasionally the nose
or a tongue or skin
create the ligatures
that bind phenomena to us.

Is sensory experience simply
a reflexive system of analogy
tumbling on top
of another analogy?
Or is it something more, such as
leaving the mind behind the eye
to make some sense
of each contour haphazardly
happening upon us?

A hawk floating.
A prickly pear, a rose.

Acknowledgments

Some of these poems appeared, in earlier versions, in my chapbook *Just Words: Homage to Roman Jakobson* (Paris: Alyscamps Press, 2019) and in Issues 3 and 4 of *The Occasional Poetry Magazine* (Dorset, UK, 2024). Thanks to the editors for permission to reprint.

Special thanks to Andrea Libin and John Ninso High for listening to these poems during "Radio Hour," and who offered their ardent support and advice. Thanks too to Richard Andersen, Marta Lopez Luaces and Julian Nangle for their ongoing belief in thinking that what I do, matters. Finally, a special thank you to my little dog Dorito who patiently sat by my side as I composed these poems, and who took me for walks so that I could truly hear the birds and see trees instead of forests.

About the Author

Christopher Sawyer-Lauçanno, 1951-2024, was widely known as a poet, translator, biographer, critic and librettist. He was the author of more than two dozen books including *Night Suite* (Talisman House), *Lorca: An Operatic Cycle in Five Parts* (Alyscamps Press), *Destruction of the Jaguar: From the Books of Chilam Balam* (City Lights), and *An Invisible Spectator: A Biography of Paul Bowles* (Grove). He lived in Turners Falls, Massachusetts.

www.ingramcontent.com/pod-product-compliance
Lightning Source LLC
Chambersburg PA
CBHW030505130626
46549CB00007B/2856